MY RECIPE BOOK

I ♥ Bakery!

CONTACT DETAILS

Baking
RECIPE

Recipe

Yield

Cooktime

Ingredients

Directions

Notes

Baking
RECIPE

Yield

Cooktime

Ingredients

Directions

IF
THERE'S
A
WHISK
THERE'S
A
WAY

Notes

Baking
RECIPE

Ingredients

Directions

Notes

Baking
RECIPE

Recipe

Yield

Cooktime

Ingredients

Directions

Notes

IF
THERE'S
A
WHISK
THERE'S
A
WAY

Baking
RECIPE

Recipe

Yield

Cooktime

Ingredients

Directions

Notes

Baking
RECIPE

Recipe

Yield

Cooktime

Ingredients

Directions

Notes

Baking
RECIPE

Recipe

Yield

Cooktime

Ingredients

Directions

Notes

Baking
RECIPE

Recipe

Yield

Cooktime

Ingredients

Directions

Notes

Baking RECIPE

Recipe

Yield

Cooktime

Ingredients

Directions

Notes

Baking
RECIPE

Ingredients

Directions

Notes

Baking
RECIPE

Recipe

Yield

Cooktime

Ingredients

Directions

Notes

Baking
RECIPE

Recipe

Yield

Cooktime

Ingredients

Directions

Notes

Baking
RECIPE

Recipe | **Yield** | **Cooktime**

Ingredients

Directions

Notes

Baking
RECIPE

Recipe

Yield

Cooktime

Ingredients

Directions

Notes

Baking
RECIPE

Recipe

Yield

Cooktime

Ingredients

Directions

Notes

Baking
RECIPE

Recipe

Yield

Cooktime

Ingredients

Directions

Notes

Baking
RECIPE

Recipe

Yield

Cooktime

Ingredients

Directions

Notes

Baking
RECIPE

Recipe

Yield

Cooktime

Ingredients

Directions

Notes

IF
THERE'S
A
WHISK
THERE'S
A
WAY

Recipe

Yield

Cooktime

Ingredients

Directions

Notes

Baking
RECIPE

Recipe

Yield

Cooktime

Ingredients

Directions

Notes

Recipe

Yield

Cooktime

Ingredients

Directions

Notes

Baking
RECIPE

Recipe

Yield

Cooktime

Ingredients

Directions

Notes

Baking
RECIPE

Recipe

Yield

Cooktime

Ingredients

Directions

Notes

Baking
RECIPE

Recipe

Yield

Cooktime

Ingredients

Directions

Notes

Baking
RECIPE

Recipe

Yield

Cooktime

Ingredients

Directions

Notes

Baking
RECIPE

Recipe

Yield

Cooktime

Ingredients

Directions

Notes

Baking
RECIPE

Recipe

Yield

Cooktime

Ingredients

Directions

Notes

Baking
RECIPE

Recipe | Yield | Cooktime

Ingredients

Directions

Notes

Baking
RECIPE

Recipe

Yield

Cooktime

Ingredients

Directions

Notes

Baking
RECIPE

Recipe

Yield

Cooktime

Ingredients

Directions

Notes

Baking
RECIPE

Recipe

Yield

Cooktime

Ingredients

Directions

Notes

Baking
RECIPE

Recipe

Yield

Cooktime

Ingredients

Directions

Notes

Baking
RECIPE

Baking
RECIPE

Recipe

Yield

Cooktime

Ingredients

Directions

Notes

Baking
RECIPE

Recipe

Yield

Cooktime

Ingredients

Directions

Notes

Baking
RECIPE

Recipe

Yield

Cooktime

Ingredients

Directions

Notes

Baking
RECIPE

Recipe

Yield

Cooktime

Ingredients

Directions

Notes

Baking RECIPE

Baking
RECIPE

Recipe

Yield

Cooktime

Ingredients

Directions

Notes

Baking
RECIPE

Recipe

Yield

Cooktime

Ingredients

Directions

Notes

Baking
RECIPE

Recipe

Yield

Cooktime

Ingredients

Directions

Notes

Baking
RECIPE

Recipe

Yield

Cooktime

Ingredients

Directions

Notes

Recipe

Yield

Cooktime

Ingredients

Directions

Notes

Baking
RECIPE

Recipe

Yield

Cooktime

Ingredients

Directions

Notes

Recipe

Yield

Cooktime

Ingredients

Directions

Notes

Baking
RECIPE

Recipe

Yield

Cooktime

Ingredients

Directions

Notes

Baking
RECIPE

Recipe

Yield

Cooktime

Ingredients

Directions

Notes

Baking
RECIPE

Recipe

Yield

Cooktime

Ingredients

Directions

Notes

Recipe

Yield

Cooktime

Ingredients

Directions

Notes

Baking
RECIPE

Recipe

Yield

Cooktime

Ingredients

Directions

Notes

Baking
RECIPE

Ingredients

Directions

Notes

Baking
RECIPE

Recipe

Yield

Cooktime

Ingredients

Directions

IF
THERE'S
A
WHISK
THERE'S
A
WAY

Notes

Baking
RECIPE

Recipe

Yield

Cooktime

Ingredients

Directions

Notes

Baking
RECIPE

Recipe

Yield

Cooktime

Ingredients

Directions

Notes

Recipe

Yield

Cooktime

Ingredients

Directions

Notes

Baking
RECIPE

Recipe

Yield

Cooktime

Ingredients

Directions

Notes

Baking
RECIPE

Recipe

Yield

Cooktime

Ingredients

Directions

Notes

Baking
RECIPE

Recipe

Yield

Cooktime

Ingredients

Directions

Notes

Baking
RECIPE

Recipe

Yield

Cooktime

Ingredients

Directions

Notes

 Baking
RECIPE

Recipe

Yield

Cooktime

Ingredients

Directions

Notes

IF
THERE'S
A
WHISK
THERE'S
A
WAY

Baking
RECIPE

Ingredients

Directions

Notes

Baking
RECIPE

Recipe

Yield

Cooktime

Ingredients

Directions

Notes

Baking
RECIPE

Ingredients

Directions

IF
THERE'S
A
WHISK
THERE'S
A
WAY

Notes

Baking
RECIPE

Recipe

Yield

Cooktime

Ingredients

Directions

Notes

Baking
RECIPE

Recipe

Yield

Cooktime

Ingredients

Directions

Notes

Baking
RECIPE

Recipe

Yield

Cooktime

Ingredients

Directions

Notes

Baking
RECIPE

Recipe | **Yield** | **Cooktime**

Ingredients

Directions

Notes

Baking
RECIPE

Recipe

Yield

Cooktime

Ingredients

Directions

Notes

Baking
RECIPE

Recipe

Yield

Cooktime

Ingredients

Directions

Notes

Baking
RECIPE

Recipe

Yield

Cooktime

Ingredients

Directions

Notes

Recipe

Yield

Cooktime

Ingredients

Directions

Notes

Baking
RECIPE

Ingredients

Directions

Notes

Baking
RECIPE

Recipe

Yield

Cooktime

Ingredients

Directions

IF
THERE'S
A
WHISK
THERE'S
A
WAY

Notes

Baking
RECIPE

Recipe

Yield

Cooktime

Ingredients

Directions

Notes

Recipe

Yield

Cooktime

Ingredients

Directions

Notes

Baking
RECIPE

Recipe

Yield

Cooktime

Ingredients

Directions

Notes

Baking
RECIPE

Recipe

Yield

Cooktime

Ingredients

Directions

Notes

Baking
RECIPE

Ingredients

Directions

Notes

Baking
RECIPE

Recipe

Yield

Cooktime

Ingredients

Directions

Notes

Recipe

Yield

Cooktime

Ingredients

Directions

IF
THERE'S
A
WHISK
THERE'S
A
WAY

Notes

Baking
RECIPE

Recipe

Yield

Cooktime

Ingredients

Directions

Notes

Baking
RECIPE

Recipe

Yield

Cooktime

Ingredients

Directions

Notes

Baking
RECIPE

Recipe

Yield

Cooktime

Ingredients

Directions

Notes

Baking
RECIPE

Ingredients

Directions

Notes

Baking
RECIPE

Recipe

Yield

Cooktime

Ingredients

Directions

Notes

Baking
RECIPE

Recipe

Yield

Cooktime

Ingredients

Directions

Notes

Baking
RECIPE

Recipe

Yield

Cooktime

Ingredients

Directions

Notes

Baking
RECIPE

Baking
RECIPE

Recipe

Yield

Cooktime

Ingredients

Directions

IF
THERE'S
A
WHISK
THERE'S
A
WAY

Notes

Baking
RECIPE

Recipe

Yield

Cooktime

Ingredients

Directions

Notes

Baking
RECIPE

Baking
RECIPE

Recipe

Yield

Cooktime

Ingredients

Directions

Notes

IF THERE'S A WHISK THERE'S A WAY

Baking
RECIPE

Recipe

Yield

Cooktime

Ingredients

Directions

Notes

Baking
RECIPE

Recipe

Yield

Cooktime

Ingredients

Directions

Notes

Baking
RECIPE

Recipe

Yield

Cooktime

Ingredients

Directions

Notes

Baking
RECIPE

Recipe

Yield

Cooktime

Ingredients

Directions

Notes

Baking
RECIPE

Recipe

Yield

Cooktime

Ingredients

Directions

Notes

Baking RECIPE

Recipe

Yield

Cooktime

Ingredients

Directions

Notes

Baking
RECIPE

Recipe

Yield

Cooktime

Ingredients

Directions

Notes

Baking
RECIPE

Recipe

Yield

Cooktime

Ingredients

Directions

Notes

Baking
RECIPE

Recipe

Yield

Cooktime

Ingredients

Directions

Notes

Baking
RECIPE

Recipe

Yield

Cooktime

Ingredients

Directions

Notes

Baking
RECIPE

Recipe

Yield

Cooktime

Ingredients

Directions

Notes

Recipe

Yield

Cooktime

Ingredients

Directions

Notes

Baking
RECIPE

Recipe

Yield

Cooktime

Ingredients

Directions

Notes

IF
THERE'S
A
WHISK
THERE'S
A
WAY

Baking
RECIPE

Recipe

Yield

Cooktime

Ingredients

Directions

Notes

Baking
RECIPE

Recipe

Yield

Cooktime

Ingredients

Directions

Notes

Baking
RECIPE

Recipe

Yield

Cooktime

Ingredients

Directions

Notes

Baking
RECIPE

Recipe

Yield

Cooktime

Ingredients

Directions

Notes

Ingredients

Directions

Notes

Baking
RECIPE

Recipe

Yield

Cooktime

Ingredients

Directions

Notes

IF THERE'S A WHISK THERE'S A WAY

Baking
RECIPE

Recipe

Yield

Cooktime

Ingredients

Directions

Notes

Baking
RECIPE

Ingredients

Directions

Notes

Baking
RECIPE

Recipe

Yield

Cooktime

Ingredients

Directions

Notes

Baking
RECIPE

Recipe

Yield

Cooktime

Ingredients

Directions

Notes

IF
THERE'S
A
WHISK
THERE'S
A
WAY

Baking
RECIPE

Recipe

Yield

Cooktime

Ingredients

Directions

Notes

Baking
RECIPE

Recipe

Yield

Cooktime

Ingredients

Directions

Notes

Recipe

Yield

Cooktime

Ingredients

Directions

Notes

Baking
RECIPE

Recipe

Yield

Cooktime

Ingredients

Directions

Notes

We hope you enjoyed our
book
As a small family company,
your feedback is very
important to us.
Please let us know
how you like our
book at :
promobileamz@gmail.com